EXPANDED EDITION
Grade
2

The *Imaginative Inventions* lesson is part of the Picture-Perfect STEM program K–2 written by the program authors and includes lessons from their award-winning series.

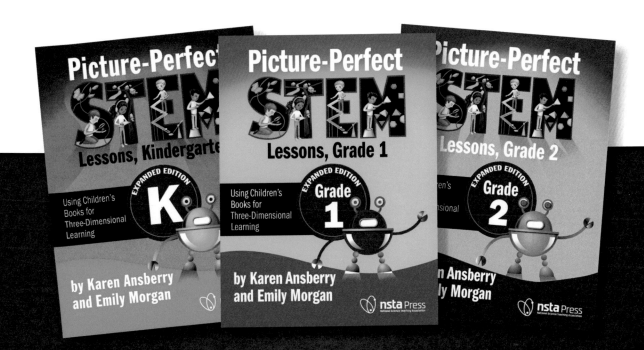

Picture-Perfect STEM Lessons, Kindergarten

Using Children's Books for Three-Dimensional Learning

EXPANDED EDITION
K

by Karen Ansberry and Emily Morgan

Picture-Perfect STEM Lessons, Grade 1

Using Children's Books for Three-Dimensional Learning

EXPANDED EDITION
Grade
1

by Karen Ansberry and Emily Morgan

nsta Press
National Science Teaching Association

Picture-Perfect STEM Lessons, Grade 2

Children's Dimensional

EXPANDED EDITION
Grade
2

n Ansberry ly Morgan

nsta Press
National Science Teaching Association

Additional information about using the Picture Perfect Science series, including key reading strategies, NGSS connections, and the BSCS 5E instructional model can be downloaded for free at:

Imaginative Inventions

Description

Learners explore the properties of matter and the engineering design process as they learn about the invention of the Frisbee, test flying discs to compare the materials they are made of and the strengths and weaknesses of how each performs, analyze data from simple tests of other toys to compare their "fun" and "safe" ratings, and design a toy of their own.

Alignment with the *Next Generation Science Standards*

Performance Expectations

2-PS1-2: Analyze data obtained from testing different materials to determine which materials have the properties that are best suited for an intended purpose.

K-2-ETS1-1: Ask questions, make observations, and gather information about a situation that people want to change to define a simple problem that can be solved through the development of a new or improved object or tool.

K-2-ETS1-2: Develop a simple sketch, drawing, or physical model to illustrate how the shape of an object helps it function as needed to solve a given problem.

Science and Engineering Practices	Disciplinary Core Ideas	Crosscutting Concepts
Planning and Carrying Out Investigations Make observations (firsthand or from media) and/or measurements to collect data that can be used to make comparisons. **Engaging in Argument from Evidence** Distinguish between opinions and evidence in one's own explanation. **Analyzing and Interpreting Data** Analyze data from tests of an object or tool to determine if it works as intended.	**PS1.A: Structure and Properties of Matter** Different properties are suited to different purposes. **ETS1.A: Defining and Delimiting Engineering Problems** A situation that people want to change or create can be approached as a problem to be solved through engineering. Before beginning to design a solution, it is important to clearly understand the problem.	**Cause and Effect** Simple tests can be designed to gather evidence to support or refute student ideas about causes. **Structure and Function** The shape and stability of structures of natural and designed objects are related to their function(s)

Continued

Science and Engineering Practices	Disciplinary Core Ideas	Crosscutting Concepts
Using Mathematics and Computational Thinking Describe, measure, and/or compare qualitative attributes of different objects and display the data using simple graphs.	**ETS1.B: Developing Possible Solutions** Designs can be conveyed through sketches, drawings, or physical models. These representations are useful in communicating ideas for a problem's solution to other people.	

Note: The activities in this lesson will help students move toward the performance expectations listed, which is the goal after multiple activities. However, the activities will not by themselves be sufficient to reach the performance expectations.

Featured Picture Books

TITLE: *Imaginative Inventions*
AUTHOR: **Charise Mericle Harper**
ILLUSTRATOR: **Charise Mericle Harper**
PUBLISHER: **Little, Brown Books for Young Readers**
YEAR: **2001**
GENRE: **Dual Purpose**
SUMMARY: *The who, what, where, when, and why of roller skates, marbles, Frisbees, and more told in rhyming verse.*

TITLE: *Flip! How the Frisbee Took Flight*
AUTHOR: **Margaret Muirhead**
ILLUSTRATOR: **Adam Gustavson**
PUBLISHER: **Charlesbridge**
YEAR: **2021**
GENRE: **Narrative Information**
SUMMARY: *This fascinating true story of how the Frisbee became a worldwide phenomenon begins on the East Coast in the 1920s, when college students were flinging "Frisbie's Pies" tins. Later, entrepreneur Fred Morrison and his wife Lu tried and failed to perfect the flying disc. Over the years, their perseverance paid off. In the 1950s, the Wham-O Corporation began manufacturing Frisbees, giving Fred and Lu lifetime royalties to the toy that would sweep the nation. For more than 20 years, Fred and Lu tried and failed to perfect a flying-disc concept. Eventually, they created what we know today as the Frisbee. Their story is full of good old-fashioned perseverance, success, and fun!*

Time Needed

NOTE: In advance, locate a suitable place outside for students to test Frisbees and other flying discs. A large field such as a soccer field is best, but a playground or even a gymnasium will work.

This lesson will take several class periods. Suggested scheduling is as follows:

Session 1: **Engage** with *Imaginative Inventions* Read-Aloud

Session 2: **Explore** with Frisbee Testing and Frisbee Testing Video (this session may take extra time depending on how long students take to test the flying discs)

Session 3: **Explain** with *Flip! How the Frisbee Took Flight* Read-Aloud and The Frisbee Design Process

Session 4: **Elaborate** with Toy Testing, Toy Testing Video, and Overall Class Testing

Session 5 and beyond: **Evaluate** with The Next Big Thing (journal, advertising posters, and optional toy fair)

Materials

For Frisbee Testing (per group of 4)

- One classic Frisbee flying disc
- One aluminum pie tin
- One foam flying disc

For Toy Testing

- 2 different inexpensive novelty toys (per student or pair of students) such as blow ball pipes, spin tops, or jumping frogs
- 1 or more child choke testers
- Fun Ratings page
- Safety Ratings page

For The Next Big Thing

- White poster paper (any size, 1 per student)
- Markers, crayons, and/or colored pencils
- Optional: Cardboard, fabric, Play-Doh, clay, recycled materials, etc. for making toy models

Spin tops, jumping frogs, and other novelty toys are available from

Oriental Trading
www.orientaltrading.com

Child Choke Testers and Floating Blow Pipe and Balls are available from

Amazon
Amazon.com

Student Pages

- Fun Ratings
- Safety Ratings
- Toy Testing
- The Next Big Thing: A Toy Design Journal
- STEM Everywhere

Background for Teachers

Inventors are problemsolvers. They think about people's problems and come up with solutions using the engineering design process. There are many variations of the design process, but in general it involves identifying and researching a problem or unmet need, brainstorming possible solutions, and then designing the solution. These steps are followed by an iterative cycle of building, testing and evaluating, and redesigning until the solution is ready to be shared (see Figure 7.1).

Exploring how toys are designed, and what they are made of, can be a relatable way for children to learn about the design process as well as the properties of materials. Toys have likely been around as long as humans have lived on Earth. Among the earliest toys were small balls or marbles made of natural materials such as stone or clay. Medieval toys were made of wood and included simple tops and cup-and-ball toys. Later, toymakers used materials such as tin and cast iron to fashion simple toys. As the Second Industrial Revolution transformed manufacturing in the 1800s, mass-produced toys became popular. In the early 1900s, walking and talking toys, toy pianos, and classics such as Lionel trains, Erector sets, the Flexible Flyer sled, Tinker Toys, Lincoln Logs, Crayola crayons, and teddy bears were introduced.

The choice of materials is a crucial part of the toy design process. By the late 1940s, Fisher-Price was the first toy company to make its entire product range in plastic. Today, 90% of toys on the market are made of plastic (source: *https://plastics-themag.com/Plastic-shakes-up-the-toy-industry*). *A Framework for K–12 Science Education* suggests that by the end of grade 2, students should understand that different materials (e.g., plastic) can be described and classified by their observable properties and that different properties (e.g., flexibility) are suited to different purposes. Toy design is an engaging way for students to explore these core science ideas.

Most students are familiar with this classic toy made entirely of plastic: the Frisbee flying disc. The evolution of the Frisbee began around the beginning of the 20th century when New England college students played with spinning "Frisbie's Pies" tins. In the 1930s, a high school student in California named Walter Frederick Morrison began spinning tin popcorn lids through the air. He and his girlfriend, Lu, tried pie plates too, then tin cake pans. He began selling the pans and thinking about ways to improve the design. He and Lu married in 1939. In 1947, when the UFO craze swept the United States, Fred came up with the idea to connect this fad with his spinning cake pan. He experimented with different materials and discovered that plastic worked much better than tin. In 1948, after several design modifications, he launched a plastic disc called the Flyin-Saucer with help from an investor named Warren Franscioni. However, the Flyin-Saucer's plastic became brittle and broke in cool temperatures. Fred didn't give up. In 1955, he and Lu used a more flexible plastic to invent the Pluto Platter.

This invention came to the attention of a California toy company called Wham-O, the makers of the famous Hula Hoop. Wham-O bought Morrison's design in 1957 and gave Fred and Lu

Figure 7.1 The Design Process

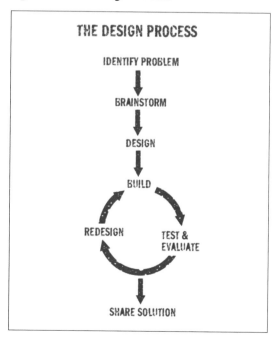

lifetime royalties. The name of their invention was soon changed to Frisbee as a nod to the Frisbie tins still in use in New England. Wham-O added a band of raised edges on the disc's surface to stabilize flight and patented the modern Frisbee in 1967. By marketing Frisbee as a new sport, the company sold more than 100 million Frisbees by 1977. The Frisbee was inducted into the National Toy Hall of Fame in 1998. Today, more Frisbees are sold every year than footballs, baseballs, and basketballs combined! Other companies have put their own spin on the original Frisbee by adding lights or using materials such as nylon, foam, and even glow-in-the-dark plastic. A more drastic design change came with the Aerobie, a flexible flying ring made of a polycarbonate core surrounded by soft rubber bumpers. Manufacturers of flying discs and other toys seek to improve their market share by improving their designs and materials.

A Framework for K–12 Science Education suggests that by the end of grade 2, students should learn how science is utilized, particularly through the engineering design process. This process begins with identifying a problem to solve and specifying the *criteria* (desired features or goals that the final product must meet). Designers of toys such as Frisbees use the same engineering design process used by many other types of inventors. They begin by exploring possible criteria for the toy such as the needs and age range of the end-user and how the toy will function (what job it will perform and how). They use methods such as watching kids at play, talking with kids to see what they want for a new or improved toy, and interviewing parents to find out the types of toys they want to purchase for their children. They do market research to find out if their idea is unique or if similar toys are already being sold. They also research availability of materials and the costs associated with mass production. Toy trends come and go, so toy designers are always thinking about unique, cost-effective, and marketable ideas for "the next big thing."

The second step is to brainstorm ideas and create multiple concepts using methods such as sketches, sculptures, and 3D computer-aided designs (CADs). Once designers settle on a concept for a toy, the next step in the process is *prototype* development. A prototype is a first full-scale and usually functional physical model of a new design. Prototyping is an essential process that takes an invention from idea to reality. In this stage, designers fine tune the toys by creating a series of physical models, using technologies such as silicone molds or 3D printing. Prototyping gives designers a real, physical model of a toy to demonstrate the actual size and shape of the product, to test materials, to try out the model with focus groups, and to help sell their idea to toy manufacturers. Each prototype is refined through the iterative steps of the design process: building, testing and evaluating, and redesigning until the toy meets the criteria and is ready to market. As this iterative cycle progresses, designers get a better idea of constraints (limitations) such as the size and weight of the toy and the availability and cost of materials.

Toy designers often observe children in controlled settings to see how they play with a new toy and to assess the toy's durability and age-appropriateness. Toys must also be tested in labs to ensure that they are safe, they work as designed, and their materials don't break, bend, or fade. The U.S. Consumer Product Safety Commission publishes rigorous standards that toys must meet in order to be sold. Toys are tested for hazards such as flammability, sharp edges, and harmful chemicals. Toys must also pass a choke test using a tool called a choke gauge, a small cylinder with an angled bottom. If a toy part can fit inside the cylinder, the toy fails and must be labeled as not for children under 3 years old.

In this lesson, students learn about disciplinary core idea (DCI) ETS1.C: Optimizing the Design Solution as they compare and test toy designs. They are engaged in the crosscutting concept (CCC) of structure and function as they explore the properties and materials of a variety of flying discs and how they function in schoolyard play. They utilize the science and engineering practice (SEP) of planning and carrying out investigations as they make firsthand observations of the flying discs and other small,

simple novelty toys to collect data that can be used to make comparisons. They use the SEPs of both analyzing and interpreting data and using mathematics and computational thinking as they analyze tests of the novelty toys to determine if the toys are both fun and safe. They then compare the toys based on their individual fun ratings and safety ratings.

Finally, in the evaluate phase of this lesson, students use the SEP of obtaining, evaluating, and communicating information as they apply their knowledge of the design process to design their own new or improved toy: The Next Big Thing. They communicate their toy designs with one another in oral and/or written forms using models, drawings, and writing, detailing each step of the process, identifying which materials might be best suited for their toy, describing ways their toy might be tested, and creating a poster to advertise their toy. You may want to have students build simple, nonworking prototypes of their toys and invite others to view the toys and advertisements at a classroom toy fair. In this way, students are mirroring the design process used by real toy designers.

Special thanks to Karl Vanderbeek, VP of Design and Human Factors at Kaleidoscope Innovation.

Learning Progressions

Below are the DCI grade band endpoints for grades K–2 and 3–5. These are provided to show how student understanding of the DCIs in this lesson will progress in future grade levels.

DCIs	Grades K–2	Grades 3–5
PS1.A: Structure and Properties of Matter	• Different properties are suited to different purposes.	• Measurements of a variety of properties can be used to identify materials.
ETS1.A: Defining and Delimiting Engineering Problems	• A situation that people want to change or create can be approached as a problem to be solved through engineering. Such problems may have many acceptable solutions. • Asking questions, making observations, and gathering information are helpful in thinking about problems. • Before beginning to design a solution, it is important to clearly understand the problem.	• Possible solutions to a problem are limited by available materials and resources (constraints). The success of a designed solution is determined by considering the desired features of a solution (criteria). Different proposals for solutions can be compared on the basis of how each one meets the specified criteria for success or how well each takes the constraints into account.

Continued

National Science Teaching Association

DCIs	Grades K–2	Grades 3–5
ETS1.B: Developing Possible Solutions	• Designs can be conveyed through sketches, drawings, or physical models. These representations are useful in communicating ideas for a problem's solution to other people.	• Research on a problem should be carried out before beginning to design a solution. Testing a solution involves investigating how well it performs under a range of likely conditions.

Source: Willard, T., ed. 2015. *The NSTA quick-reference guide to the* NGSS: *Elementary school.* Arlington, VA: NSTA Press.

 # engage

Imaginative Inventions Read-Aloud

 ### Making Connections: Text to World

Show the cover of the book *Imaginative Inventions*, and introduce the author and illustrator. *Ask*

? What is an invention? (something that is made to meet a need or solve a problem)

? What is the difference between an invention and a discovery? (An invention is something that is created; a discovery is something that is found for the first time. For example, Ben Franklin discovered that lightning is electrical current, but he invented the lightning rod.)

? How are new things invented?

? Who invents new things?

? What is the first step when inventing something new?

? What is the final step when inventing something new?

 ### Turn and Talk

Next, build connections to the author by reading the inside flap of the book about author Charise Mericle Harper's favorite invention ("… muffins, which taste a lot like cake, but you get to eat them for breakfast!") Ask students to first discuss the following question with a partner, then share with the whole class.

? What do you think is the greatest invention ever and why? (Answers will vary.)

Connecting to the Common Core
Reading: Informational Text
KEY IDEAS AND DETAILS: 2.1

 ### Inferring

Tell students that the book *Imaginative Inventions* may not contain the invention they chose as the greatest, but it contains a lot of great inventions! Skipping pages 6–7 about the Frisbee, select several of the toys and other inventions in the book to read about. As you read each poem aloud, hide the illustrations and leave out the name of the invention. Instead, say "this invention." Ask students to make inferences about the identity of each invention using clues from the text. They can turn to a

partner and whisper their guesses as you read. After reading each two-page spread, reveal the illustrations and name of the invention and read the facts in the sidebar on the right-hand side of each spread.

> **SEP: Obtaining, Evaluating, and Communicating Information**
> Communicate information or design ideas and/or solutions with others in oral and/or written forms using models, drawings, writing, or numbers that provide details about scientific ideas, practices, and/or design ideas.

Then tell students that inventors think about people's unmet "needs" and "wants"(desires) and come up with ways to meet them. Ask students to identify the need or desire that each invention met. For example, a piggy bank met a need for a fun way to save loose change. A flat-bottomed paper bag met a need for a bag that could be filled while it was standing up. Potato chips met a customer's desire for a thinner fry.

Next, read pages 6–7 about the invention of the Frisbee and ask students to infer which toy the poem is describing. Reveal the toy and read the facts in the sidebar. Then ask students to identify the need or desire that the Frisbee met.

> **CCC: Structure and Function**
> The shape and stability of structures of natural and designed objects are related to their function(s).

Finally, hold up a classic Frisbee disc and *ask*

? Has anyone ever played with a Frisbee? (Answers will vary.)

? What is the function of a Frisbee? In other words, what is it designed to do? (to soar

COMPARING FLYING TOYS

through the air, to be used for fun, to be used for sports, etc.)

? What about its structure, or the way it is shaped, helps it do its job? (It is round, flat, smooth, lightweight, aerodynamic, etc.)

? What is a Frisbee made of? (plastic)

? Why is a Frisbee made of plastic? Why not rock, or glass, or cloth? (Students may laugh at this idea, but it will help them realize that a Frisbee is made of plastic because plastic has the right properties for the job. Plastic is not too hard, or sharp, or soft, etc. It is the best material to use for making Frisbees.)

? What is fun about playing with a Frisbee? (Answers will vary.)

? What is not so fun, or not so safe, about playing with a Frisbee? (Some Frisbees are hard for kids to throw or catch, a person could get hurt if hit by a Frisbee, a Frisbee could get stuck on a roof or sink in water, a Frisbee could be lost in the dark, and so on.)

? What are some ways that the shape or materials of the Frisbee could be changed to make it more fun, safer, or meet another need or desire? (Answers will vary.)

explore

Frisbee Testing

Tell students that instead of coming up with completely new inventions, inventors often think of ways to make an old one better. They might give the invention different features or make it out of different materials. A good example of this involves the improvements made to the classic Frisbee disc. Have students explore the improvements to the Frisbee's design. Provide each group of four a classic Frisbee, an aluminum pie tin, and a foam flying disc. Caution students not to throw them in the classroom!

As students are making observations of the flying discs, *ask*

? What do you notice about these designs? (They have the same basic shape but different colors, sizes, and profiles.)

? What do you wonder about these designs? (Answers will vary.)

Have groups put the flying discs in order of least fun to most fun. Have students hold up the flying disc they ranked as most fun. *Ask*

? What observations support your claims? In other words, how did you decide which would be the most fun? (Answers will vary.)

Then have each group hold up the disc they think would be the most fun and compare to other groups.

Next, have groups hold up the flying disc they ranked as least fun. *Ask*

? What observations support your claims? In other words, how did you decide which would be the least fun? (Answers will vary.)

Then have each group hold up the disc they think would be the least fun and compare to other groups.

Next, have groups put the flying discs in order of least safe to most safe. Have students hold up the flying disc they ranked as most safe. *Ask*

? What observations support your claims? In other words, how did you decide which would be the most safe? (Answers will vary.)

TESTING THE FLYING DISCS

Then have each group hold up the disc they think would be the most safe and compare to other groups.

Next, have groups hold up the flying disc they ranked as least safe. *Ask*

? What observations support your claims? In other words, how did you decide which would be the least safe? (Answers will vary.)

Then have each group hold up the disc they think would be the least safe and compare to other groups.

> **SEP: Engaging in Argument from Evidence**
> Distinguish between opinions and evidence in one's own explanation.

Next, tell students that the best way to make these claims is to actually play with the toys. *Ask*

? What observations could you make as you play with the flying discs to support your claims about the fun rankings? In other words, what could you observe in order to compare them? (Answers might include observing how well they fly, how far they fly, or how easy they are to throw or catch in comparison to one another.)

? What observations could you make as you play with the flying discs to support your claims about the safety rankings of the flying discs? (Answers might include observing how hard it hits your hand, how much control you have over where it goes, etc.)

> **CCC: Cause and Effect**
> Simple tests can be designed to gather evidence to support or refute ideas about causes.

Frisbee Testing Video

Tell students that testing is always done on toys, both by toy companies before the toy is sold and by end-users (people who buy or play with the toy) after the toy is on the market. Many students have likely seen toy testing videos on YouTube. Show the first 2:37 of the video "What is the Best Frisbee for Backyard Throwing?" (see "Websites") and ask students to listen and watch for what the man in the video wants to test. Then *ask*

? What kinds of things will he be testing for each flying disc? (how fast and far it flies, how straight and level it flies, how easy it is to throw, how comfortable it is to hold, etc.)

? How many of you would like to be flying disc testers? (It is likely that all students will want to be testers!)

Next, announce to the class that they will be going outside to test the flying discs! Caution them not to leave the playground, not to throw the discs onto a roof, and to use care when throwing so a flying disc doesn't hit someone. Remind them to be encouraging to one another, as some children may not have had much experience playing with Frisbees.

> **SEP: Planning and Carrying Out Investigations**
> Make observations (firsthand or from media) and/or measurements to collect data that can be used to make comparisons.

Students can choose what criteria they will use to determine what constitutes "fun" and "safe." Students will be collecting qualitative data using relative scales (easier to throw than, farther than, straighter than, faster than, etc.). They won't be measuring and recording distance or time in the air because of the difficulty involved. Some students may not have much experience throwing flying discs, so reassure them that it's OK if they

aren't perfect with their throwing or catching. The goal is to explore ways to test toys and to have fun!

Then go outside to the playground or, even better, a large grassy field. Students should spread out and work in groups of four. Make sure all students in each group have at least one turn throwing and one turn trying to catch a flying disc. Continue until every group has had a chance to test each variation of flying disc (or until you run out of time).

 **Turn and Talk**

Return to the classroom and have each student turn and talk with a student from another group to compare their observations. Then *ask*

? Do you want to revise your initial claims about fun and safety based on new evidence? In other words, how would your rankings change?

? Which disc was the most comfortable to hold?

? Which one was the easiest to throw or catch?

? Which one had the longest, straightest, or most level flight?

? What material is each disc made of? (The pie tin is metal, the Frisbee is made of rigid plastic, and the other is made of soft foam.)

? How do those materials make them more or less fun?

? How do those materials make them more or less safe?

? Which one was the most fun? The least fun?

? Which one was the most safe? The least safe?

? Which one would you be most likely to buy? Why?

? How do you think the Frisbee was invented?

Tell students that they might be surprised to learn that the pie tin had something to do with how the Frisbee was invented!

explain

Flip! How the Frisbee Took Flight Read-Aloud

In advance, make a poster-sized version of The Design Process (Figure 7.1), which features the model used on the PBS show *Design Squad Global*. Two different color versions are available to print at *www.pictureperfectscience.com* (see Resources and click on the Extras tab).

Then *ask*

? Who did we learn designed the original Frisbee? (In the book *Imaginative Inventions*, students learned that the Frisbee was designed by a man named Walter, identified in the sidebar as Walter Frederick Morrison.)

? What did he first use as a flying disc? (a pie tin)

Tell students that you have another book that gives more background on how this inventor used the design process to go from a pie tin to a Frisbee. Introduce the author and illustrator of the book *Flip! How the Frisbee Took Flight*. Tell students that the inventor is referred to by his middle name (Fred) in this book. As you read the book aloud, ask students to listen for examples of how Fred Morrison used the design process.

The Frisbee Design Process

After reading, ask students to cite examples from the book for each step of the design process. They may need prompting to connect each step to an example from the text. Use Table 7.1 to help you facilitate this discussion.

Table 7.1 The Frisbee Design Process

Step	What it Means	Examples from the book *Flip!*
Identify Problem	Figure out something people need or want.	(page 7) Fred wanted something fun to do in the backyard after dinner.
Brainstorm	Come up with lots of ideas that might work.	(page 7) Fred tried using a tin popcorn lid. (page 8) Fred tried pie plates. (page 9) Fred tried cake pans.
Design	Imagine what the solution might look like and draw it.	(page 15) Fred imagined a flying tin with rounded edges or raised ridges. (*Note:* We don't know from reading if he just imagined it or also drew pictures of the solution.)
Build, Test, and Evaluate; Redesign	Build the solution, see if it works, make changes, test it again, and repeat until you are satisfied with the solution.	(page 19) Fred and Warren created the first Flyin-Saucer out of lightweight, pliable (bendable) plastic. (page 21) In cool temperatures, the Flyin-Saucer broke. (page 22) Fred and Lu tried a new design with a more flexible plastic and renamed it the Pluto Platter. It didn't break!
Share Solution	Tell others about the solution and try to use or sell it.	(page 22) Fred sold the Pluto Platter at fairs. (pages 24-26) A toy company called Wham-O took interest and bought the design from Fred and Lu. (page 29) Wham-O renamed it Frisbee and sales shot up. Millions of Frisbees have been sold.

Discuss the materials that Fred used while designing and improving the Frisbee. *Ask*

? What materials did he try? (metal, plastic, flexible plastic)

? How did those materials work? (The metal was not safe. The first plastic he tried broke when it got cold. The more flexible plastic was safe and did not break.)

Tell students that since Wham-O started making Frisbees, many improvements have been made using other materials such as foam, glow-in-the-dark plastic, and nylon. You may want to show them photos or real examples of improved Frisbees and discuss the benefits of each type of material. For example, foam makes the toy soft and safe, glow-in-the-dark plastic makes it easy to see at night, and nylon makes it foldable and portable.

elaborate

Toy Testing

After discussing the Frisbee design process from the book *Flip!, ask*

? How do you think Fred Morrison tested his flying discs? (He played with them to see how

well they flew, how durable they were, and how safe they were.)

? Why do toy designers and toy companies need to test toys? (to see if the toys work and if they are fun and safe)

Toy Testing Video

Tell students that real kids are the best toy testers! Many toy companies give children toys to test and observe their reactions to them. Kids can tell toy designers if a toy is truly fun, but safety is important, too. Toy companies are required by law to do safety tests on their toys. Explain that a magazine called *Good Housekeeping* runs a toy-testing lab where engineers test toys for safety and kids test toys for fun. Have them watch the 2:40 minute video called "Toy Testing at *Good Housekeeping*" (see "Websites") to observe a toy testing lab in action.

After watching the toy testing video, *ask*

? What did you notice?

? What do you wonder?

? Would you like to be a toy tester?

SEP: Planning and Carrying Out Investigations
Make observations to collect data that can be used to make comparisons

---

Tell students that they are going to have a chance to be toy testers! On the board, write the name of one of the toys they will be testing (see Materials) and label it "Toy A." Write the name of the other toy on the board and label it "Toy B." Then pass out a Toy Testing student page to each student. Point out that the student page has four different parts. Explain that first, they will play with both toys. In Part 1, they will draw and label the toys. In Part 2, they will rate the toys for how fun they are. In Part 3, they will rate the toys for how safe they are. In Part 4, they will decide which toy they would prefer to buy.

Next, give each student or pair of students both toys to test. Allow them several minutes to play with the toys. Then have them put the toys on their desks so they can complete the student page. For Part 1, ask them to determine what material(s) the toys are made of (they may need help with this) and to draw and label the materials and parts of each toy.

For Part 2, ask them to decide how fun the toys are (they may need more time to play with them!). *Ask*

? How did you decide what counted as fun when you tested the flying discs? (Answers will vary.)

? Can we use these same criteria for fun as we test and compare the toys? (Answers will vary.)

The "fun" rating will be relative. For example, a blow ball pipe might be considered "very fun" as compared to a "sort of fun" jumping frog or spinning top. However, to compare a blow ball pipe to a video game might not be fair!

For Part 3, ask students to consider the safety of each toy's materials and parts. Explain that most toys come with warning labels and/or directions for using the toy safely. These labels (if they are included on the toys or their packaging) can help them compare the safety of the toys. Return to students' initial criteria for "safe" and make connections between students' ideas and safety labels on toys.

Then discuss the possible risks of toys. Explain that toy testers look for sharp parts that could hurt a child. For this activity, students can gently run their fingers around the toy to assess if there are any pieces of plastic or other materials that could poke a child. Remind them to use caution! Toy testers also check for choking hazards. Babies and young children often put things in their mouths. If a toy is too small, or contains small parts, it could be a choking hazard for children under 3 years old. Show students a choke tester, a tool that can be used to determine whether toys have parts that young children can swallow. To use the choke tester, students can drop the toy or toy part into the clear cylinder. If it falls in, it is not safe because it could get caught in a child's throat. The diameter

of the tube is 1 ¼ inch, about the same size as a 3-year-old's throat. Students can use the warning labels, assessment of sharp parts, choke testing results, and anything else that might indicate the toy is unsafe to come up with their ratings. (Keep the choke tester accessible during the toy testing so students can use it to test the toys.) *Ask*

? How did you decide what counted as safe when you tested the flying discs?

? Can we use these same criteria for safety as we test and compare the toys? (Answers will vary, but students will likely want to add "sharp edges" and the choking test to their criteria.)

Then have students give a safety rating for each toy. Finally, students can compare the fun and safety ratings of the two toys to determine which toy they personally would prefer to buy.

Have them fill out the Toy Testing student page as shown:

1. Play with the toys! Then draw each toy below and label its parts and materials.

Toy A Drawing	Toy B Drawing

2. Give each toy a fun rating:

	Toy A			Toy B		
Fun	☹ not fun	😐 sort of fun	☺ very fun	☹ not fun	😐 sort of fun	☺ very fun

3. Use the choke tester to test each toy and check for sharp parts. Then give each toy a safety rating:

	Toy A			Toy B		
Safety	☹ not safe	😐 sort of safe	☺ very safe	☹ not safe	😐 sort of safe	☺ very safe

4. Which toy would you prefer to buy? Why?

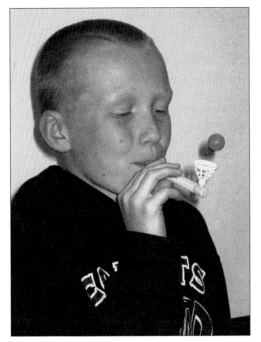

TESTING A BLOW BALL PIPE

WARNING LABEL FOR A BLOW BALL PIPE

Have students briefly share some of their ratings and discuss the criteria they used to come up with them. Point out that not everyone gave the toys the same ratings. Then *ask*

? Do you think companies use only one toy tester? (No. It is good to have more than one opinion about a toy.)

Overall Class Ratings

Discuss the idea that toy companies don't take just one person's opinion about a toy. They collect many people's opinions before making changes to the toy or before deciding to sell it in stores. Project the Fun Ratings page onto a screen. Point out the parts of the graph: the title, the x-axis label, the y-axis label, and the box with lines for summarizing the class ratings for Toy A and Toy B. Tell students that the graph will help them make a conclusion about the toy by showing everyone's ratings. Use a colored marker to color in the box for Toy A on the key. By a show of hands, count the number of "not fun" ratings and draw a bar using the color for Toy A. Then count the "sort of fun" and "very fun" ratings. Next, use a different-colored marker

to color in the box for Toy B on the key. By a show of hands, count the number of "not fun" ratings and draw a bar using the color for Toy B. Repeat for the other two ratings.

Have students look carefully at all of the ratings on the graph. Have them come up with an overall class fun rating for Toy A by *asking*

? Which fun rating did Toy A get most often?

Record that rating in the class rating box at the top of the graph. Then have students come up with an overall class fun rating for Toy B by *asking*

? Which fun rating did Toy B get most often?

Record that rating in the class rating box at the top of the graph.

SAMPLE FUN RATINGS WHOLE-CLASS GRAPH

SEP: Using Mathematics and Computational Thinking
Describe, measure and/or compare qualitative attributes of different objects and display the date using simple graphs.

Project the Safety Rating page onto a screen. Follow the same process to come up with an overall class safety rating for both toys. Finally, ask students to compare the scores of both toys by comparing the class ratings. *Ask*

? Which toy scored higher for fun?

? Which toy scored higher for safety?

? What material is each toy made of? (Answers will vary depending on the toys used.)

? How do those materials make the toys more or less fun?

? How do those materials make the toys more or less safe?

? Which toy would you prefer to buy? Why?

? Which toy do you think a toy company would want to sell? Why?

? How could you improve on either of the toys?

evaluate

The Next Big Thing

Reread pages 24–25 in the book *Flip!*, where the California toy company Wham-O took interest in Fred's invention. Tell students that toy trends come and go, and toy companies like Wham-O are always looking for "the next big thing" to sell to their customers. *Ask*

? What other famous toy did Wham-O sell? (The book mentioned the Hula Hoop. Students may know of other Wham-O toys such as the Slip 'N Slide.)

? Has anyone ever played with a Hula Hoop? (Answers will vary.)

Tell students that, like the Frisbee, there have been many improvements to toys such as the Hula Hoop and the Slip 'N Slide. Often, toy manufacturers improve on existing toys rather than invent brand-new ones. Show the vintage Wham-O Frisbee & Hula Hoop commercial from the 1960s (see the "Websites") and *ask*

? What improvement was made to the Hula Hoop? (They gave it a "shoop shoop" sound.)

? How many different Frisbees were sold at the time this commercial was made? (seven)

? Is the Frisbee still a "big thing"? (Yes. Remind students that, according to the book *Imaginative Inventions*, more Frisbees have been sold than footballs, baseballs, and basketballs combined!)

? What are some of today's "big" (popular or bestselling) toys? (Answers will vary.)

? Would you like to design the next big thing in toys? (Students will likely say yes!)

Connecting to the Common Core
Writing
RESEARCH TO BUILD KNOWLEDGE: 2.7

Tell students that they are going to have the opportunity to be toy designers. Pass out The Next Big Thing student pages to each student. Tell them that they will be using the journal to guide them through the design process of creating "The Next Big Thing" – a new and improved toy! (Optional: You may want to have students build models of their toy designs.)

The journal takes students through each step of the design process:

1. **Identify Problem:** Figure out what kids need or want in a toy. Ask other students about a toy they like to play with. What do they think could be improved to make it more fun, more safe, or work better?

2. **Brainstorm:** Draw and/or write your ideas for improving some of the popular toys you discussed earlier (or other toys you have played with).

3. **Design:** Choose one of your ideas for a new and improved toy. Draw and label the toy in the box. Give the new and improved toy a name. Think about the materials it would be made of. What materials would make it fun? What materials would make it safe?

4. **Build, Test and Evaluate, Redesign:** How would you test the new and improved toy to decide if it were fun and safe?

5. **Share the Solution:** Tell others about the new and improved toy. Make an advertisement to sell it!

   - **3 points:** Make a drawing of the new and improved toy, label its parts, and give it a new name.

   - **2 Points:** Describe the material that would be used to make the toy and why you chose that material.

   - **1 Point:** Explain why the new and improved toy is more fun and/or safe than the original.

For fun, the students can include a catchy slogan on their advertisement to help sell the toy to consumers.

You may want to share and discuss a vintage Frisbee ad to give the students some ideas for their advertising poster (see "Websites"). Project the ad onto a screen and *ask*

? What does the ad say is new and improved about this Frisbee? (It has a new design.)

? What are some of the features of this Frisbee? (It flies like a plane, spins like a gyroscope, curves, boomerangs, flies straight, and comes in three colors.)

? Does the ad tell what the Frisbee is made of? (No.)

? What does the ad say about safety? (The Frisbee is soft, safe, and unbreakable.)

THE NEXT BIG THING

? How does the ad help sell the Frisbee? (It makes it seem new and exciting, it has pictures, it tells what it does, and it describes all of its unique features.)

? Does the ad have a catchy slogan – a short and memorable phrase used in advertising? ("If it's not Wham-O, it's not a Frisbee!")

SEP: Obtaining, Evaluating, and Communicating Information
Communicate information or design ideas and/or solutions with others in oral and/or written forms using models, drawings, writing, or numbers that provide detail about scientific ideas, practices, and/or design ideas.

Next, students can create three-dimensional, nonworking scale models of their toys out of cardboard, fabric, Play-Doh, clay, recycled materials, and so on. Consider holding a toy fair and inviting parents or other students to your classroom. In the design world, toy fairs are exciting conventions where toy industry professionals showcase their toy lines and reveal new products. Your students will enjoy displaying their journals, toy advertisements, and models for the toy fair "attendees." Have guests do a gallery walk through the classroom, using sticky notes to post questions and positive critiques on the students' posters. Writing on sticky notes encourages interaction, and the comments provide immediate feedback for the "exhibitors."

STEM Everywhere

Give students the STEM Everywhere student page as a way to involve their families and extend their learning. They can do the activity with an adult helper and share their results with the class. If students do not have access to these materials or the internet at home, you may choose to have them complete this activity at school.

Opportunities for Differentiated Instruction

This box lists questions and challenges related to the lesson that students may select to research, investigate, or innovate. Students may also use the questions as examples to help them generate their own questions. These questions can help you move your students from the teacher-directed investigation to engaging in the science and engineering practices in a more student-directed format.

Extra Support

For students who are struggling to meet the lesson objectives, provide a question and guide them in the process of collecting research or helping them design procedures or solutions.

Extensions

For students with high interest or who have already met the lesson objectives, have them choose a question (or pose their own question), conduct their own research, and design their own procedures or solutions.

After selecting one of the questions in this box or formulating their own questions, students can individually or collaboratively make predictions, design investigations or surveys to test their predictions, collect evidence, devise explanations, design solutions, or examine related resources. They can communicate their findings through a science notebook, at a poster session or gallery walk, or by producing a media project.

Research

Have students brainstorm researchable questions:

? What are the world records for Frisbee flight?

? Who invented the Aerobie and how is it different or better than the Frisbee?

? Who invented one of your favorite toys and how did they do it?

Investigate

Have students brainstorm testable questions to be solved through science or math:

? Test two different flying discs. Which flies the greatest distance?

? Does the size of a flying disc affect how far it goes?

? Which material is best for a flying disc that floats on water?

Innovate

Have students brainstorm problems to be solved through engineering:

? Can you make a flying disc out of cardboard or another safe material?

? Can you design a carrying case for a flying disc?

? Can you make a flying disc light up or make sound?

Websites

What is the Best Frisbee for Backyard Throwing?
www.youtube.com/ watch?v=3lRNsXOT9TM

Toy Testing at *Good Housekeeping*
www.youtube.com/ watch?v=Cd94h9wumbA

Wham-O Frisbee & Hula Hoop Commercial (1960s)
www.youtube.com/ watch?v=tsJ9fwhFzE8

Vintage Frisbee Ad
https://2.bp.blogspot.com/-_W-EASPFvFU/UKaBSwLzPul/ AAAAAAAAF0o/bCJBt7mhhdl/s640/ Frisbee_Adwhamo.png

More Books to Read

Barton, C. 2016. *Whoosh! Lonnie Johnson's super-soaking stream of inventions*. New York: Charlesbridge.
Summary: This picture book biography tells the story of Lonnie Johnson, an African American NASA scientist turned entrepreneur who invented the super-soaker water gun.

Ford, G 2016. *The marvelous thing that came from a spring: The accidental invention of the toy that swept the nation*. New York: Atheneum Books for Young Readers.
Summary: Using whimsical dioramic illustrations and simple, informative text, this book tells the story of how engineer Richard James accidently invented the iconic Slinky.

Kirkfield, V. 2021. *From here to there: Inventions that changed the way the world moves*. New York: Clarion Books.
Summary: This collective biography tells the stories of the visionaries who revolutionized the way people travel.

Rustad, M. 2015. *What is it made of? Noticing types of materials*. Minneapolis: Millbrook Press.
Summary: Colorful, cartoonish characters; lively narrative text; and fact-filled insets tell the story of a "treasure hunt" in Ms. Sampson's class. But the students aren't searching for real treasure – they are on the hunt for cloth, rock, glass, metal, and all of the different materials that make up objects in their school.

St. George, J. 2002. *So you want to be an inventor?* New York: Puffin Books.
Summary: This witty look at some of the world's best-known (and lesser-known) inventors features short, entertaining profiles and trivia accompanied by humorous illustrations.

Taylor, B. 2003. *I wonder why zippers have teeth: And other questions about inventions*. New York: Kingfisher.
Summary: "What did people use before they had refrigerators?" and "Where do inventors get their ideas?" are some of the questions answered in this intriguing question-and-answer book about common household inventions.

Name: _____

Fun Ratings

Toy A ☐ Class Rating: _____
Toy B ☐ Class Rating: _____

25
20
15
10
5
0

Number of Ratings

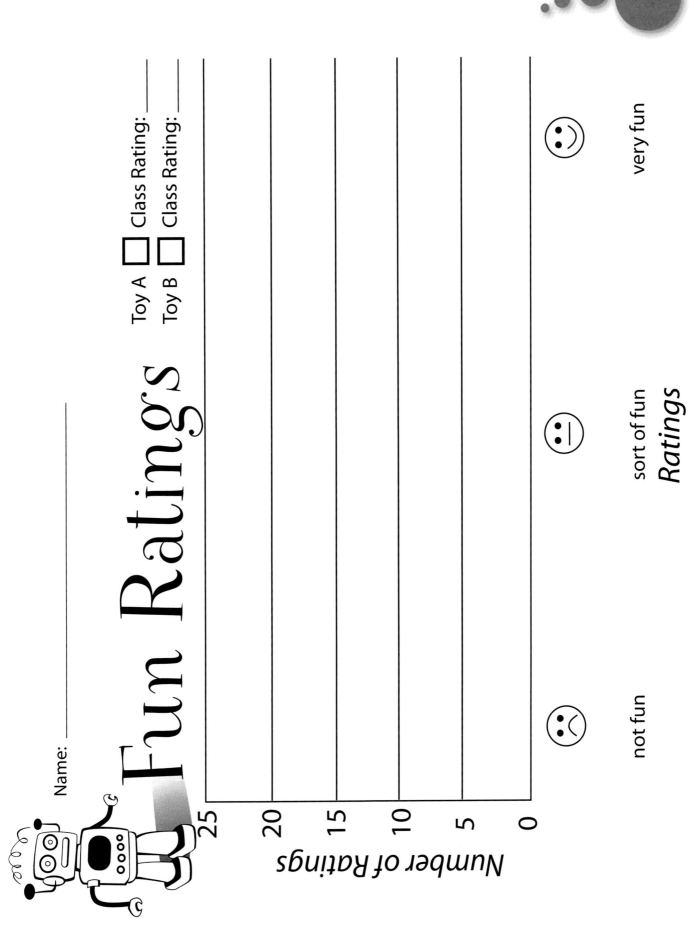

not fun   sort of fun   very fun

Ratings

Name: _____

Safety Ratings

Toy A ☐ Class Rating: _____
Toy B ☐ Class Rating: _____

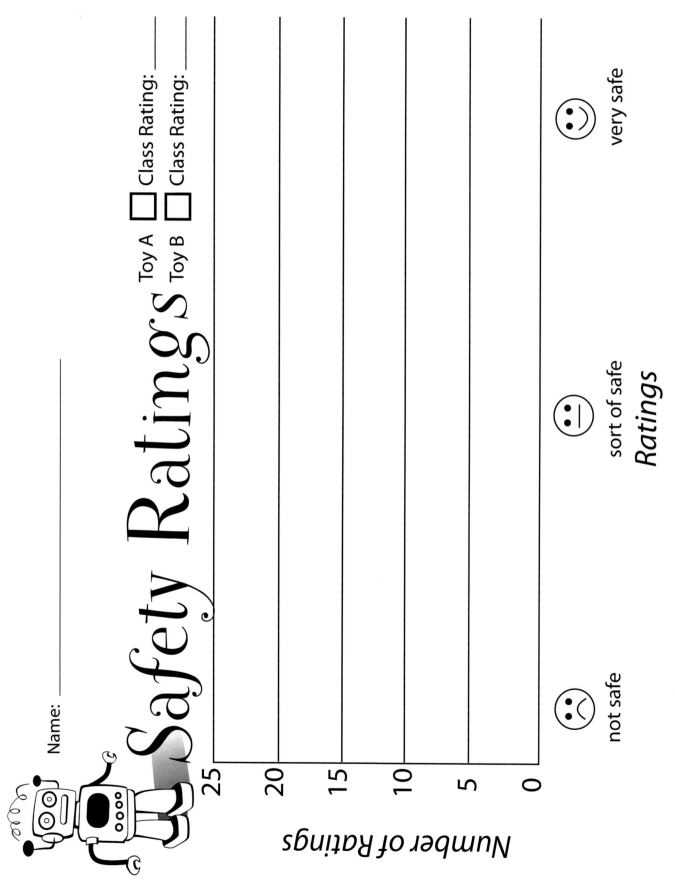

25
20
15
10
5
0

Number of Ratings

not safe — sort of safe — very safe

Ratings

National Science Teaching Association

Name: _____

Toy Testing

1. Play with the toys!
   Then draw each toy below and label its parts and materials.

Toy A Drawing	Toy B Drawing

2. Give each toy a fun rating:

Toy A	Toy B
☹ not fun 😐 sort of fun 🙂 very fun	☹ not fun 😐 sort of fun 🙂 very fun

3. Use the choke tester to test each toy and check for sharp parts.
   Then give each toy a safety rating:

Toy A	Toy B
☹ not safe 😐 sort of safe 🙂 very safe	☹ not safe 😐 sort of safe 🙂 very safe

4. Which toy would you prefer to buy? Why? _____

   _____

The Next Big Thing
A Toy Design Journal

Name: _____

National Science Teaching Association

1. **Identify Problem:** Figure out what kids need or want in a toy. Ask other students about a toy they like to play with. What do they think could be improved to make it more fun, more safe, or work better?

Student's Name	Toy	Improvement

2. **Brainstorm:** Draw and/or write your ideas for improving some of the toys above (or other toys you have played with).

3. **Design:** Choose one of your ideas for a new and improved toy. Draw and label the toy in the box below. Give the new and improved toy a name. Think about the materials it would be made of.

Name of original toy: _____

Name of new and improved toy: _____

What materials would the new and improved toy be made of? Why?

_____

_____

_____

_____

4. **Build, Test and Evaluate, Redesign:** How would you test the new and improved toy to decide if it is fun and safe?

_____

_____

_____

_____

5. **Share the Solution:** Tell others about the new and improved toy. Make an advertisement to sell it!

3 Points: Make a drawing of the new and improved toy, label its parts, and give it a new name.

3   2   1   0

2 Points: Describe the material that would be used to make the toy and why you chose that material.

2   1   0

1 Point: Explain why the new and improved toy is more fun and/or safe than the original.

1   0

For fun, include a catchy slogan!

Total Points_____/6

Comments: _____

_____

_____

Name: _____

STEM Everywhere

At school, we have been learning about **the design process**. This is a process used by inventors and other creative people to solve problems. To find out more, ask your learner questions such as:

- What did you learn?
- What was your favorite part of the lesson?
- What are you still wondering?

 At home, you can watch a video called "100 Years of Toys" and then talk about how toys have changed over the years: *www.youtube.com/watch?v=EDAPaEVr1Hk*

After Watching

Adult Helper: List some toys you liked to play with as a child.

_____   _____

_____   _____

_____   _____

Together: Brainstorm ideas for improving the toys above by making them safer or more fun. Then choose one toy and improve it.

Name of toy: _____

Learner: Draw and label the new and improved toy in the box below.

National Science Teaching Association